G
W O R K
D

THEOLOGY OF WORK
MARKETPLACE MINISTRY 101

By : John Fryters

Theology of Work – Marketplace Ministry 101
School of Theology and Ministry
by J.A. Fryters, Ph.D., ICADC (ret)

Printed in the United States of America

ISBN 9781626970267

Unless otherwise indicated, all Scripture quotations are taken from **The New Century Version** of the Bible. "Scriptures quoted from The Holy Bible, New Century Version,

Books referenced:

The Cape Town Commitment, by Chris Wright

Christ our Reconciler, Tim Keller, Rebecca Manley Pippert, John Piper, Chris Wright, and others.

The Covenant of Lausanne, references related to "Releasing Kings for Ministry in the Marketplace" and quotations at the end of each chapter, used with special permission

Biblical Life College & Seminary
1100 Spur Dr Ste 180, P.O. Box 588
Marshfield, MO 65706-0588
Phone *(417) 859-0881* **Fax** *(417) 468-2037*
E-mail : biblicallife@centurytel.net **Web site :** http://www.biblical-life.com

www.xulonpress.com

ACKNOWLEDGMENTS

Many, many people have contributed in ways known and unknown to the writing of this book. First and foremost, I would like to thank my wife Hannelore whose patience, obviously given to her by the Holy Spirit, has been remarkable. She dealt with the computer glitches, printer disconnects, tea breaks, and, most of all, my frustrations with today's technology. It is only because she loves me that this book/course manual finally saw the light...

Then I would like to thank all of CHAKAM's TOW students in Peru, the new Republic of South Sudan, and Northern Canada for their candid remarks throughout the various seminars and workshops. Somehow some of these remarks became a part of this curriculum, if not in word, certainly in spirit.

Thank you so much to Bakke Graduate University's Theology of Work Grant Program. The program was established in 2006 by the Mustard Seed Foundation and is administered by BGU. Dr. Lowell Bakke approved our initial grant application.

TOW grant recipients create and offer accredited (formal) theology of work educational programs for future pastors that will enable them to effectively steward the callings and vocations of their congregants who are working in the marketplace and non-church centered environments. Other recipients create and offer continuing education (non-formal) programs for both pastors and marketplace leaders.

Of course, my thanks also goes to Biblical Life College and Seminary in Marshfield, Missouri, particularly to its Chancellor, Dr. Michael Lake, Th.D., D. Psy., for allowing this to become an official course offering in BLCS's School of Theology and Ministry.

Most of all, I would like to thank my personal Lord and Savior, Jesus of Nazareth, for keeping me, loving me and embracing me through the process of compiling and writing these course materials.

ABOUT THE AUTHOR

Dr. **John J.A. Fryters** is the Founder and current Transition Adviser of CHAKAM School of the Bible Inc. in Prince Albert, Saskatchewan with currently (2013) 12 sub-campuses in Canada (Saskatchewan), the Republic of South Sudan, Ghana, Uganda, Tanzania and Peru (www.worldoutreach.ca). CHAKAM, in collaboration with South Sudan Humanitarian Action Development Agency, also built and is operating a Comprehensive Technical Training

Institute in the new Republic of South Sudan.

Dr. Fryters has been on the International Faculty of Biblical Life College and Seminary for about 12 years.

Dr. Fryters has also been an addiction therapist for about 30+ years. He is an Internationally Certified Alcohol and Drug Counsellor (ICADC – now retired). He founded a number of addiction assessment and treatment services in Canada and is widely sought after as a specialist speaker and consultant in his field. He has served as a Director on the Board of Governors of the Ontario Addiction Research Foundation, and as the Chair of the International Advisory Board of The Journal (a renowned magazine for addiction management specialists). Until recently, he served as a public representative on the Saskatchewan College of Physicians and Surgeons.

Dr. Fryters has a special interest in volunteering and in community development. He has served on countless Boards and Committees dealing with addictions, homelessness, family violence, private vocational schools, halfway house management, nursing, palliative and hospice care, legal assistance to the poor, etc...

He received Jesus at the age of thirty followed by the Baptism of the Holy Spirit about 4 days later. About eleven years after salvation, he answered God's call to minister the Gospel. Since then, he developed two Bible Training Institutes - CHAKAM (see above) being one of them, and planted a number of churches. Currently, besides directing CHAKAM, he pastors a small teaching church in Prince Albert called Under The Juniper Tree Chapel and he directs three other independent ministries (Centre for Excellence in International Development, the Association of Biblical Life Educators in Canada, and Jubilation Residential Centres – see www.worldoutreach.ca).

Dr. Fryters, his wife, Rev. Hannelore Fryters, and their 13-year old granddaughter Jenine live in Prince Albert, Northern Saskatchewan, Canada.

ABOUT THIS BOOK

This book is presented in the format of an actual course manual/ workbook – an official course offering through the School of Theology and Ministry of Biblical Life College and Seminary (http://www.biblical-life. com). Those interested in taking this course for official educational credits, should contact BLCS at biblicallife@ centurytel.net.

This book can not be read or under-stood without having your Bible in your other hand.

1. Class Description

The class is designed to provide an elementary, basic understanding of the Theology of Work for the purposes of this manual called "Marketplace Ministry 101". The class also provides a Biblical basis for the Theology of Work.

2. Class Perspective

A Biblical Theology of Work includes at least two critical God-given mandates for mankind : a) the Creation Mandate of Genesis 1 & 2 to subdue or rule the earth with God; and b) the Redemption Mandate of Matthew 28 to reconcile people and the earth to God.

Much of Bible College, Seminary and even Church training has been focused on and modeling the Redemption Mandate, but little focus has been given to the Creation Mandate. The Theology of Work is not new, but it is infrequently taught in our seminaries and other pastoral training places. As a result, pastors rarely teach or discuss Theology of Work principles within the church.

3. Collateral Reading

"Releasing KINGS for Ministry in the Marketplace" by John S. Garfield & Harold R. Eberle. Published by Worldcast Publishing, P.O. Box 10653, Yakima, WA 98909-1653 USA. ISBN 978-1-882523-26-9

4. Module Requirements and Assignments

- At the beginning of each lesson there will be reading assignments. The student is to complete the required reading before proceeding with the lesson.

- The manual is designed using a programmed-learning format. With this format, the student is challenged to retain and recall information presented in the manual through various kinds of repetition. The questions in each lesson will generally precede the answer. It is fashioned this way to challenge you before reading specific paragraphs within the lesson. Then each lesson is followed by review questions. The student should answer these questions upon completion of carefully reviewing of each lesson's content in general. (*)

- The student is to use these questions to prepare for the Final Examination.

- Final Examination : there will be one Final Examination for this manual. The questions will be taken from both the lecture materials as well as those covered in the list of the review questions in the syllabus.

- Collateral Reading : the student is to read through the book required for the collateral reading and write one 10 page, typed and double-spaced essay on the topic *"How Are The Principles, Taught In Releasing Kings, Going To Assist Me In My Market Place Ministry ?"*

(*) An additional review of the presented materials can be accessed by ordering lectures on DVD. Please check in the back of this book for an appropriate order form. These DVD's are not necessarily required to complete the above described work.

TABLE OF CONTENT

Lesson One

From the God in Genesis to the God of the Great Commission to us and The Lausanne Covenant – Part One

After the Fall, though appropriately dealing with Adam and Eve, God immediately set a plan in motion speaking to the snake : ***"I will make you and the woman enemies to each other. Your descendants will be enemies. One of her descendants will crush your head, and you will bite his heel." (Gen 3:15)***.

Jesus came and fulfilled Gen 3:15. However, before He left the earth, Jesus told His followers (and us) : ***"All power in heaven and on earth is given to me. So go and make followers of all people in the world. Baptize them in the name of the Father and the Son and the Holy Spirit. Teach them to obey everything that I have taught you, and I will be with you always, even until the end of this age." (Matt 28:18-20)***

So, the process set in motion by Jesus, the process of evangelization (spreading the Good News) was immediately started in earnest. Throughout its history, the church made a number of serious and not so serious, and sometimes flawed, attempts at evangelization.

One of the more serious attempts was the Lausanne Congress on World Evangelization, held in Lausanne, Switzerland, from July 16th – 25th, 1974. This Congress brought together 4000+ evangelists, missionaries, mission leaders, theologians, pastors and national church leaders from over 150 nations.

A drafting committee headed by Dr. John R.W. Stott incorporated the ideas of the main speakers and submissions of hundreds of participants. On the final day, Dr. Billy Graham, the leaders, and participants signed a document, called **The Lausanne Covenant,** in a moving public ceremony.

The freshly printed document spread quickly around the world. Evangelists shared it with new converts. Missionaries shared it in newly planted churches. Denominations studied its themes and challenges. By the mid 70's to the early 80's many other churches and agencies had already adopted it as their statement of faith. By the 1980's virtually every major evangelical mission agency in North America, and many in other countries, had endorsed the Covenant to replace or supplement their own statements of faith.

In this way, the fifteen tightly packed sections of the Covenant quickly spread the essence of Lausanne's emphasis on biblical world evangelization, and helped spark what became known as "the Lausanne Movement". An Asian theologian wrote : "History may show this Covenant to be the most significant ecumenical confession on evangelism that the church has ever produced".

All content of this course "Theology of Work – Market Place Ministry 101" is effectively filtered through the Biblical Foundations which make up "the Lausanne Covenant". Consequently, understanding the Theology of Work means that one needs to really understand this important Covenant which I will quote verbatim (the questions are not part of this Covenant, but part of the learning methods in this book) :

THE LAUSANNE COVENANT

INTRODUCTION

We, members of the Church of Jesus Christ, from more than 150 nations, participants in the International Congress on World Evangelization at Lausanne, praise God for His great salvation and rejoice in the fellowship He has given us with Himself and with each other. We are deeply stirred by what God is doing in our day, moved to penitence by our failures and challenged by the unfinished task of evangelization. We believe the gospel is God's good news for the whole world, and we are determined by His grace to obey Christ's commission to proclaim it to every person and to make disciples of every nation. We desire, therefore, to affirm our faith and our resolve, and make public our covenant.

1. THE PURPOSE OF GOD

We affirm our belief in the one eternal God, Creator and Lord of the world, Father, Son and Holy Spirit, who governs all things according to the purpose of His will.

- **How do we deny our calling
  and fail our mission ?**

_____

_____

_____

_____

_____

_____

He has been calling out from the world a people for Himself, and sending His people back into the world to be His servants and His witnesses, for the extension of His kingdom, the building up of Christ's body, and the glory of His name. We confess with shame that we have often denied our calling and failed in our mission, by becoming conformed to the world or by withdrawing from it. Yet we rejoice that even when borne by earthen vessels the gospel is still a precious treasure. To the task of making that treasure known in the power of the Holy Spirit we desire to dedicate ourselves anew.

(Isa 40:28; Matt 28:19; Eph 1:11; Acts 15:14; John 17:6, 18; Eph 4:12; Rom 12:2; 1 Cor 5:10; 2 Cor 4:12)

2. THE AUTHORITY AND POWER OF THE BIBLE

We affirm the divine inspiration, truthfulness and authority of both Old and New Testament Scriptures in their entirety as the only written Word of God, without error in all that it affirms, and the only infallible rule of faith and practice.

- **To whom is the message of the Bible addressed ?**

_____

_____

_____

_____

_____

_____

We also affirm the power of God's word to accomplish His purpose of salvation. The message of the Bible is addressed to all men and women. For God's revelation in Christ and in Scripture is unchangeable. Through it the Holy Spirit still speaks today. He illumines the minds of God's people in every culture to perceive its truth freshly through their own eyes and thus discloses to the whole Church ever more of the many-colored wisdom of God.

(2 Tim 3:16; 2 Pet 1:12; Isa 55:11; Rom 1:16; 1 Cor 1:21; John 10:35; Matt 5:17, 18; Jude 3; Eph 1:17, 18)

3. THE UNIQUENESS AND UNIVERSALITY OF CHRIST

We affirm that there is only one Savior and only one gospel, although there is a wide diversity of evangelistic approaches. We recognize that everyone has some knowledge of God through His general revelation in nature. But we deny that this can save, for people suppress the truth of their unrighteousness. We also reject as derogatory to Christ and the gospel every kind of syncretism and dialog which implies that Christ speaks equally through all religions and ideologies. Jesus Christ, being Himself the only God-man, who gave Himself as the only ransom for sinners, is the only mediator between God and people. There is no other name by which we must be saved.

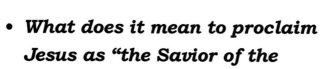

- **What does it mean to proclaim Jesus as "the Savior of the world" ?**

_____

_____

_____

_____

_____

_____

All men and women are perishing because of sin, but God loves everyone, not wishing that any should perish but that all should repent. Yet those who reject Christ repudiate the joy of salvation and condemn themselves to eternal separation from God. To proclaim Jesus as "the Savior of the world" is not to affirm that all people are either automatically or ultimately saved, still less to affirm that all religions offer salvation in Christ. Rather it is to proclaim God's love for a world of sinners and to invite everyone to respond to Him as Savior and Lord in the wholehearted personal commitment of repentance and faith. Jesus Christ has been exalted above every name; we long for the day when every knee shall bow to Him and every tongue shall confess Him Lord.

(Gal 1:6-9; Rom 1:18-32; 1 Tim 2:5, 6; Acts 4:12; John 3:16-19; 2 Pet 3:9; 2 Th 1:7-9; John 4:42; Matt 11:28; Eph 1:20, 21; Phil 2:9-11)

4. THE NATURE OF EVANGELISM

To evangelize is to spread the good news that Jesus Christ died for our sins and was raised from the dead according to the Scriptures, and that as the reigning Lord He now offers the forgiveness of sins and the liberating gift of the Spirit to all who repent and believe.

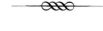

• *What is evangelism itself ?*

_____

_____

_____

_____

_____

_____

Our Christian presence in the world is indispensable to evange-lism, and so is that kind of dialog whose purpose is to listen sensitively in order to understand. But evangelism itself is the proclamation of the historical, biblical Christ as Savior and Lord, with a view to persuading people to come to Him personally and so be reconciled to God. In issuing the gospel invitation we have no liberty to conceal the cost of discipleship. Jesus still calls all who would follow Him to deny themselves, take up their cross, and identify themselves with His new community. The results of evangelism include obedience to Christ, incorporation into His Church and responsible service in the world.

(1 Cor 15:3, 4; Acts 2:32-39; John 20:21; 1 Cor 1:23; 2 Cor 4:5; 2 Cor 5:11, 20; Luke 14:25-33; Mark 8:34; Acts 2:40, 47; Mark 10:43-45)

5. CHRISTIAN SOCIAL RESPONSIBILITY

We affirm that God is both the Creator and the Judge of all. We therefore should share His concern for justice and reconciliation through human society and for the liberation of men and women from every kind of oppression.

• *As it relates to social concern, why do some of us have to express penitence ?*

_____

_____

_____

_____

_____

_____

_____

Because men and women are made in the image of God, every person, regardless of race, religion, color, culture, class, sex or age, has an intrinsic dignity because of which he or she should be respected and served, not exploited. Here too we express penitence both for our neglect and for having sometimes regarded evangelism and social concern as mutually exclusive. Although reconciliation with other people is not reconciliation with God, nor is social action evangelism, nor is political liberation salvation, nevertheless we affirm that evangelism and socio-political involvement are both part of our Christian duty. For both are necessary expressions of our doctrines of God and man, our love for our neighbor and our obedience to Jesus Christ. The message of salvation implies also a message of

judgment upon every form of alien-
ation, oppression and discrimina-
tion, and we should not be afraid to
denounce evil and injustice wherever
they exist. When people receive Christ
they are born again into His kingdom,
and must seek not only to exhibit but
also to spread its righteousness in
the midst of an unrighteous world.
The salvation we claim should be
transforming us in the totality of our
personal and social responsibilities.
Faith without works is dead.

*(Acts 17:26, 31; Gen 18:25; Ps 45:7;
Isa 1:17; Gen 1:26, 27; Lev 19:18;
Luke 6:27, 35; Jas 3:9; John 3:3, 5;
Matt 5:20; Matt 6:33; 2 Cor 3:18; Jas
2:14-26)*

6. THE CHURCH AND EVANGELISM

We affirm that Christ send His redeemed people into the world as the Father sent Him, and that this calls for a similar deep and costly penetration of the world. We need to break out of our ecclesiastical ghettos and permeate non-Christian society.

- *With what should the "church" not be identified ?*

_____

_____

_____

_____

_____

_____

_____

In the Church's mission of sacrificial service, evangelism is primary. World evangelization required the whole Church to take the whole gospel to the whole world.

The Church is at the very center of God's cosmic purpose and is His appointed means of spreading the gospel. But a church which preaches the cross must itself be marked by the cross. It becomes a stumbling block to evangelism when it betrays the gospel or lacks a living faith in God, a genuine love for people, or scrupulous honesty in all things including promotion and finance. The church is the community of God's people rather than an institution, and must not be identified with any particular culture, social or political system, or human ideology.

(John 17:18; John 20:21; Matt 28:19, 20; Acts 1:8; Acts 20:27; Eph 1:9, 10; Eph 3:9-11; Gal 6:14, 17; 2 Cor 6:3, 4; 2 Tim 2:19-21; Phil 1:27)

7. COOPERATION IN EVANGELISM

We affirm that the Church's visible unity in truth is God's purpose. Evangelism also summons us to unity, because our oneness strengthens our witness, just as our disunity undermines our gospel of reconciliation.

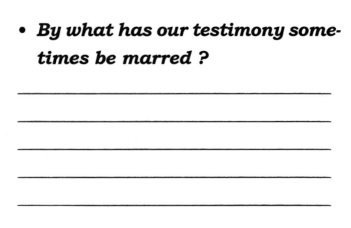

- *By what has our testimony sometimes be marred ?*

_____

_____

_____

_____

_____

_____

We recognize, however, that organizational unity may take many forms and does not necessarily forward evangelism. Yet we who share the same biblical faith should be closely united in fellowship, work and witness. We confess that our testimony has sometimes been marred by sinful individualism and needless duplication. We pledge ourselves to seek a deeper unity in truth, worship, holiness and mission. We urge the development of regional and functional cooperation for the furtherance of the Church's mission, for strategic planning, for mutual encouragement, and for the sharing of resources and experience.

(Eph 4:3; John 17:21, 23; John 13:35; Phil 1:27)

Lesson Two

From the God in Genesis to the God of the Great Commission to us and The Lausanne Covenant – Part Two

THE LAUSANNE COVENANT

8. CHURCHES IN EVANGELISTIC PARTNERSHIP

We rejoice that a new missionary era has dawned. The dominant role of Western missions is fast disappearing. God is raising up from the younger churches a great new resource for world evangelization, and is thus demonstrating that the responsibility to evangelize belongs to the whole body of Christ. All churches should therefore be asking

God and themselves what they should be doing both to reach their own area and to send missionaries to other parts of the world. A reevaluation of our missionary responsibility and role should be continuous.

- ***Why should churches and parachurch agencies engage in constant self-examination ?***

_____

_____

_____

_____

_____

_____

_____

Thus a growing partnership of churches will develop and the universal character of Christ's Church will be more clearly exhibited. We also thank God for agencies which labor in Bible translation, theological education, the mass media, Christian literature, evangelism missions, church renewal and other specialist fields. They too should engage in constant self-examination to evaluate their effectiveness as part of the Church's mission.

(Rom 1:8; Phil 1:5; Phil 4:15; Acts 13:1-3; 1 Th 1:6-8)

9. THE URGENCY OF THE EVANGELISTIC TASK

More than 2,700 million people, which is more than two-thirds of all humanity, have yet to be evangelized. We are ashamed that so many have been neglected; it is a standing rebuke to us and to the whole Church. There is now, however, in many parts of the world an unprecedented receptivity to the Lord Jesus Christ.

• *What is our main goal ?*

_____

_____

_____

_____

_____

_____

We are convinced that this is the time for churches and para-church agencies to pray earnestly for the salvation of the unreached and to launch new efforts to achieve world evangelization. A reduction of foreign missionaries and money in an evangelized country may sometimes be necessary to facilitate the national church's growth in self-reliance and to release resources for unevangelized areas. Missionaries should flow ever more freely from and to all six continents in a spirit of humble service. The goal should be by all available means and at the earliest possible time, that every person will have the opportunity to hear, understand, and receive the good news. We cannot hope to attain this goal without sacrifice. All of us are shocked by the poverty of millions and disturbed by the injustices which cause it. Those of us who live in affluent circumstances accept our duty to develop a simple life-style in order to contribute more generously to both relief and evangelism.

(Mark 16:15; John 9:4; Matt 9:35-38; Isa 58:6, 7; Jas 2:1-9; 1 Cor 9:19-23; Jas 1:27; Matt 25:31-46; Acts 2:44, 45; Acts 4:34, 35)

10. EVANGELISM AND CULTURE

The development of strategies for world evangelization calls for imaginative pioneering methods. Under God, the result will be the rise of churches deeply rooted in Christ and closely related to their culture. Culture must always be tested and judged by Scripture.

• *In the past, what did missions export with the gospel and what was the result ?*

_____

_____

_____

_____

_____

_____

Because men and women are God's creatures, some of their culture is rich in beauty and goodness. Because they are fallen, all of it is tainted with sin and some of it is demonic. The gospel does not presuppose the superiority of any culture to another, but evaluates all cultures according to its own criteria of truth and righteousness, and insists on moral absolutes in every culture. Missions have all too frequently exported with the gospel an alien culture and churches have sometimes been in bondage to culture rather than to Scripture. Christ's evangelists must humbly seek to empty themselves of all but their personal authenticity in order to become the servants of others, and churches must seek to transform and enrich culture, all for the glory of God.

(Mark 7:8, 9, 13; Gen 4:21, 22; 1 Cor 9:19-23; Phil 2:5-7; 2 Cor 4:5)

11. EDUCATION AND LEADERSHIP

We confess that we have sometimes pursued church growth at the expense of church depth, and divorced evangelism from Christian nurture. We also acknowledge that some of our missions have been too slow to equip and encourage national leaders to assume their rightful responsibilities.

- ***What kind of training programs need to be developed for pastors and laity ?***

_____

_____

_____

_____

_____

_____

Yet we are committed to indigenous principles, and long that every church will have national leaders who manifest a Christian style of leadership in terms not of denomination but of service. We recognize that there is a great need to improve theological education, especially for church leaders. In every nation and culture there should be an effective training program for pastors and laity in doctrine, discipleship, evangelism, nurture and service.

Such training programs should not rely on any stereotyped methodology but should be developed by creative local initiatives according to biblical standards.

(Col 1:27, 28; Acts 14:23; Titus 1:5, 9; Mark 10:42-45; Eph 4:11, 12)

12. SPIRITUAL CONFLICT

We believe that we are engaged in constant spiritual warfare with the principalities and powers of evil, who are seeking to overthrow the Church and frustrate its task of world evangelization. We know our need to equip ourselves with God's armor and to fight this battle with the spiritual weapons of truth and prayer.

- ***What does it mean "not to be immune to worldliness of thought and action" ?***

_____

_____

_____

_____

_____

_____

For we detect the activity of our enemy, not only in false ideologies outside the Church, but also inside it in false gospels which twist Scripture and put people in the place of God. We need both watchfulness and discernment to safeguard the biblical gospel. We acknowledge that we ourselves are not immune to worldliness of thought and action, that is, to a surrender to secularism. For example, although careful studies of church growth, both numerical and spiritual, are right and valuable, we have sometimes neglected them. At other times, desirous to ensure a response to the gospel, we have compromised our message, manipulated our hearers through pressure techniques, and become unduly preoccupied with statistics or even dishonest in our use of them. All this is worldly. The Church must be in the world; the world must not be in the Church.

(Eph 6:12; 2 Cor 4:3, 4; Eph 6:11, 13-18; 2 Cor 10:3-5; 1 Jn 2:18-26; 1 Jn 4:1-3; Gal 1:6-9; 2 Cor 2:17; 2 Cor 4:2; John 17:15)

13. FREEDOM AND PERSECUTION

It is the God-appointed duty of every government to secure conditions of peace, justice and liberty in which the Church may obey God, serve the Lord Christ, and preach the Gospel without interference.

• ***Freedom of thought, conscience, to practice and propagate religion should be according to these two things ?***

_____

_____

_____

_____

_____

_____

We therefore pray for the leaders of the nations and call upon them to guarantee freedom of thought and conscience, and freedom to practice and propagate religion in accordance with the will of God and as set forth in The Universal Declaration of Human Rights. We also express our deep concern for all who have been unjustly imprisoned, and especially for those who are suffering for their testimony to the Lord Jesus. We promise to pray and work for their freedom. At the same time we refuse to be intimidated by their fate. God helping us, we too will seek to stand against injustice and to remain faithful to the gospel, whatever the cost. We do not forget the warnings of Jesus that persecution is inevitable.

(1 Tim 2:1-4; Col 3:24; Acts 4:19; Acts 5:29; Heb 13:1-3; Luke 4:18; Gal 5:11; Gal 6:12; Matt 5:10-12; John 15:18-21)

14. THE POWER OF THE HOLY SPIRIT

We believe in the power of the Holy Spirit. The Father sent His Spirit to bear witness to His Son; without this witness ours is futile. Conviction of sin, faith in Christ, new birth and Christian growth are all His work.

- ***What is a church that is not a missionary church ?***

_____

_____

_____

_____

_____

_____

Further, the Holy Spirit is a missionary spirit; thus evangelism should arise spontaneously from a Spirit-filled church. A church that is not a missionary church is contradicting itself and quenching the Spirit. Worldwide evangelization will become a realistic possibility only when the Spirit renews the Church in truth and wisdom, faith, holiness, love and power. We therefore call upon all Christians to pray for such a visitation of the sovereign Spirit of God that all His fruit may appear in all His people and that all His gifts may enrich the body of Christ. Only then will the whole Church become a fit instrument in His hands, that the whole earth may hear His voice.

(Acts 1:8; 1 Cor 2:4; John 15:26, 27; John 16:8-11; 1 Cor 12:3; John 3:6-8; 2 Cor 3:18; John 7:37-39; 1 Th 5:19;

Ps 85:4-7; Gal 5:22, 23; Rom 12:3-8; 1 Cor 12:4-31; Ps 67:1-3)

15. THE RETURN OF CHRIST

We believe that Jesus Christ will return personally and visibly, in power and glory, to consummate His salvation and His judgment. This promise of His coming is a further spur to our evangelism, for we remember His words that the gospel must first be preached to all nations.

- *What needs to happen between Christ's ascension and return ?*

_____

_____

_____

_____

_____

We believe that the interim period between Christ's ascension and return is to be filled with the mission of the people of God, who have no liberty to stop before the end. We also remember His warning that false Christs and false prophets will arise as precursors

of the final Antichrist. We therefore reject as a proud, self-confident dream that notion that people can ever build a utopia on earth. Our Christian confidence is that God will perfect His kingdom, and we look forward with eager anticipation to that day, and to the new heaven and earth in which righteousness will dwell and God will reign forever. Meanwhile we rededicate ourselves to the service of Christ and of people in joyful submission to His authority over the whole of our lives.

(Mark 14:62; Heb 9:28; Mark 13:10; Matt 28:20; Acts 1:8-11; Mark 13:21, 23; 1 John 2:18; 1 John 4:1-3; Luke 12:32; Rev 21:1-5; 2 Pet 3:13; Matt 28:18)

CONCLUSION

Therefore, in the light of this our faith and our resolve, we enter into a solemn covenant with God and with each other, to pray, to plan and to work together for the evangelization of the whole world. We call upon others to join us. May God help us by His grace and for His glory to be faithful to this our covenant! Amen. Alleluia!

THE LAUSANNE COVENANT

Lesson Three

Key Elements of The Lausanne Covenant to remember while we study Marketplace Ministry

Reading Assignment – read the Foreword by John L. Sanford, the Preface, and the Introduction of *"Releasing Kings for Ministry in the Marketplace"* by John S. Garfield and Harold R. Eberle, pages ix – xii, 1-7

- **According to the Founder of Elijah House, John Sanford, what does** "Releasing Kings for Ministry in the Marketplace" **aim to do ?**

_____

_____

_____

- **Where is the real work of the ministry and how is it done ?**

_____

_____

_____

- **After reading the Introduction, give a short description of the contemporary version of the word "King"?**

_____

_____

_____

———— ⚬⚬⚬ ————

"But when the Holy Spirit comes to you, you will receive power. You will be my witnesses – in Jerusalem, in all of Judea, in Samaria, and in every part of the world." (Acts 1:8)

Within our study of Marketplace Ministry, it is important to remember crucial parts of The Lausanne Covenant, and more importantly its Biblical Foundations, as it relates to pulling the gospel outside of our institutions and into the world at large (or marketplace).

Here is a quick review of these crucial elements :

- we are **moved to penitence by our failures**

- we are **challenged by the unfinished task of evangelization**
- the gospel is God's good news **for the whole world**
- obey Christ's commission to **proclaim it to every person** and **to make disciples of**
- **every nation**
- the message of the Bible is **addressed to all men and women**
- he illumines the minds of God's people **in every culture**
- there is **a wide diversity of evangelistic approaches**
- God loves everyone, **not wishing that any should perish** but that all should repent
- to **invite everyone** to respond to him as Savior and Lord in the wholehearted

- personal commitment of repentance and faith
- to evangelize is **to spread** the good news
- evangelism itself is **the proclamation** of the historical, biblical Christ as Savior and
- Lord, **with a view to persuading people to come to Him personally and so be reconciled to God**
- share His concern for justice and reconciliation **throughout human society**
- when people receive Christ they are **born again into His kingdom**, and must seek
- not only to exhibit but also **to spread its righteousness in the midst of an unrighteous world**
- Christ sends His redeemed people **into the world**

- this **calls for a** similar deep and **costly penetration of the world**
- and **permeate non-Christian society**
- the whole Church **to take** the whole gospel **to the whole world**
- His appointed **means for spreading the gospel**
- we pledge ourselves to seek **a deeper unity in** truth, worship, holiness and **mission**
- a **new missionary era** has dawned
- all churches should therefore be asking God and themselves what they should be
- doing both **to reach their own area** and **to send missionaries to other parts of the world**
- we are **ashamed that so many have been neglected**

- **pray** earnestly **for the salvation of the unreached** and **to launch new efforts to**
- **achieve world evangelization**
- by all available means and at the earliest possible time, **that every person will have**
- **the opportunity to hear, understand and receive the good news**
- we cannot hope to attain this goal without **sacrifice**
- calls for **imaginative pioneering methods**
- churches must **seek to transform and enrich culture**
- should be developed by **creative local initiatives according to biblical standards**
- we ourselves are **not immune to worldliness of thought and action**, that is, **to a**
- **surrender to secularism**

- the **Church must be in the world; the world must not be in the Church**
- to remain faithful to the gospel, **whatever the cost**
- the **Holy Spirit is a missionary spirit**
- worldwide evangelization **will become a realistic possibility only when the Spirit**
- **renews the Church** in truth and wisdom, faith, holiness, love and power
- only then will the whole Church become a fit instrument in his hands, that **the whole**
- **earth may hear His voice**
- the interim period between Christ's ascension and return is to be filled with **the**
- **mission of the people of God, who have no liberty to stop**

before the end

- to work together for **the evangelization of the whole world**

All of these quotes make it very
clear that The Lausanne Covenant
really emphasized the importance of
the "Great Commission" as spoken
by God in Matt 28:18-20 and in Acts
1:8. While the many laws of the Torah
and the two great commandments
given by Jesus in Matt 22:37-40 are
very important (and, of course, we
should live our lives according to
them), Jesus, in Matt 28:18-20, made
it extremely clear that we, believers,
have been given His authority to teach
others whatever He taught us (i.e. to
make disciples) in our own sphere of
influence and all across the world.

The Apostle Paul, in 2 Cor 10:13,
makes it very clear that God has given

us all "a sphere of influence (work)" and it is clear that most of us (i.e. those not called into direct five-fold ministry according to Eph 4:11) need to work within that sphere to bring Jesus to others and subsequently make disciples.

****

What interests me is the perceived lack of connection between church and work. The average Christian spends less than 2% of their waking time at church. Yet, the church puts most of its energy and resources into that 2% and very little into the world of daily work.
Allistair Mackenzie

****

We want to go to this
mp3   1 Cor 11.1 ←
00:42:00 → 1:25 -

Lesson Four

"Follow me for I follow Jesus"

What did Paul know ?

Reading Assignment – read Part I – Kings in the Marketplace, Priests in the Church of *"Releasing Kings for Ministry in the Marketplace"* by John S. Garfield and Harold R. Eberle, pages 9 – 13

- ***Who are "Kings" and what is the intended role of Kings ?***

_____

_____

_____

_____

_____

_____

Ever come across a Scripture which sounds strange and even question-able or controversial ? Yes, of course you have. Here is one of those verses :

"Follow my example, as I follow the example of Christ." (1 Cor 11:1)

Who does Paul think he is ? How arrogant can you be ? Ask me to try to follow Christ and (maybe) I will, but to follow a man, I have to think about it twice.... And which other minister would even dare to ask the same what Paul is asking : "Follow my example, as I follow the example of Christ" ?

Why didn't Paul tell the believers in the church of Corinth to just follow Christ ? There must have been a good reason to say what he did say. Moreover, Paul seemed to understand what God wanted him to do as he keeps on repeating that same message in his letters to various New Testament churches :

Again to the church in Corinth, he said : ***"For though you may have ten thousand teachers in Christ, you do not have many fathers. Through the Good News I became your father in Christ Jesus, so I beg you, please follow my example."*** ***(1 Cor 4:15-16)***

Not only is he asking the believers, he is "begging" them to follow his example. Also, he is adding that they would not only be following Paul, the

Apostle, but rather Paul, their spiritual father through the Gospel.

To the church in Thessalonica, he said : ***"We had the right to ask you to help us, but we worked to take care of ourselves so we would be an example for you to follow." (II Th 3:9)*** and ***"And you became like us and like the Lord." (I Th 1:6a)***

Of course, it is important to observe the two Scriptures together because in the first Scripture Paul makes reference to him (and the other leaders) as "working" and that this "working" should be an example for the believers in Thessalonica to follow. And in the second Scripture Paul tells the believers that they first became like him (and the other leaders) and then, watch carefully, like the Lord. Can we draw any conclusions ?

It also needs to be stated that, in this context, the word "follow" is the Greek word *"mimetes"* which provide the root for the English words "mime', "to mimic" and "to imitate". So, we are to imitate our spiritual leaders (spiritual fathers) as they are imitating Christ.

Paul's statement to the believers in Thessalonica is again repeated to the believers in Philippi : ***"Brothers and sisters, all of you should try to follow my example and to copy those who live the way we showed you." Phil 3:17***

He now is extending the following not only to himself but also to those who are already following (uses the word copying) him (and, of course, the other leaders).

Although there is no full agreement among scholars on who wrote Hebrews, many believe that Paul was the author.

This manual is not the correct place to argue the authorship of Hebrews. Assuming that Paul indeed wrote this Holy Ghost inspired book, he adds :
"We do not want you to become lazy. Be like those who through faith and patience will receive what God has promised." Heb 6:12

The author add one additional element and it is the element of "laziness". The author obviously concludes that receiving God's promises, through faith and patience, can not be obtained if one is lazy. This theme is also repeated in the two letters by Paul to the church in Thessalonica.

While all of these Scriptures tell us to imitate our spiritual leaders as they, in turn, imitate Christ, none of them tell us that our spiritual leaders are perfect in any way, infallible or even imitate Christ correctly. Paul was a man, the apostles of old were men, and we, ministers today, are men. The only thing the Holy Spirit tells us, through Paul, is that we are to imitate Christ so that, in turn, those we are ultimately spiritually responsible for can imitate us.

No matter what, the statement made by Paul in 1 Cor 11:1 still remains a tall order!!! One can only made a similar statement if one is indeed following Christ....

There are a few explanations why Paul said what he said.

1. Although Jesus had just left the earth to sit on the right hand of the Father, Paul knew that people's memory is usually short and their faith not strong enough. If he would ask them to follow an unseen God, they

might have difficulty. A step in between would be to follow an earthly leader (spiritual father).

2. Paul had met Jesus face to face on the road to Damascus and received "direct" instructions from Jesus. This, most likely, also happened on other occasions (1 Cor 11:23). If the instruction in 1 Cor 11:1 was not directly received from Jesus, it was certainly received by the inspiration of the Holy Spirit as all Scriptures are inspired by the Holy Spirit.

3. There is no doubt that Paul was one of the first Bible scholars. He not only studied and knew the Torah, but from his writings it is clear that he studied Jesus (the New Testament), most likely under the direct guidance of other apostles.

King Agrippa 1:27   80
I've been true to the gospel

REPETITION IS THE MOTHER OF ALL LEARNING

Listening/Viewing Assignment – in order to further strengthen your learning of this topic, teaching through a DVD series is available to the readers. Please check in the back of this book for a form to order a copy of this DVD recording.

****

Work is the expenditure of energy (manual or mental or both) in the service of others, which brings fulfillment to the worker, benefit to the community and glory to God
Dr. John Stott

****

Handwritten notes:
mp3 01:25 — 1:53
     1:54 — 3:18

Lesson 5
Part 3

Something
burns inside
me
Not Quicken

Lesson Five

A forgotten attribute of God – "Work"

Reading Assignment – read Part I : Kings in the Marketplace, Priests in the Church, Chapters 1 – 6, and Conclusion in *"Releasing Kings for Ministry in the Marketplace"* by John S. Garfield and Harold R. Eberle, pages 15 – 50

- **In what capacity did Nehemiah achieve what Ezra could not accomplish ?**

_____

_____

_____

_____

- **Name briefly four characteristics of Kings ?**

_____

_____

_____

_____

- **Name four things that make a King tick ?**

_____

_____

_____

_____

_____

• *Pastors function primarily
in _____ and Kings in
_____ ?*

_____

_____

_____

_____

_____

*When will we receive a return on
our investments (quote Scripture) ?*

_____

_____

_____

_____

_____

In 1 Cor 11:1 Paul tells us : *"Follow
my example, as I follow the example
of Christ."* So, what was the example

of Christ. We immediately think about
Christ's (God's) attributes such as
love, peace, mercy, justice, forgiveness, faithfulness, etc... Would we
ever think that a "work ethic" might
be one of God's attributes ?

An in-depth study of the Word
clearly shows us that "work ethic" is
indeed one of God's attributes. How
can God's work ethic be described ?
Here are some observations :

1. The term "God" and "work" are
almost synonymous.

Commentator Finis Dake tells us
that God, through His Word, men-
tions the concept of "work" some 416
times. Scriptures related to "work"
are mentioned 116 times. The word
"works" appears 235 times.

God, in the Scriptures, made it clear that we are to work. This is going to be highlighted in more detail in Lesson Seven. However, here are a few selections :

"You will sweat and work hard for your food. Later you will return to the ground, because you were taken from it. You are dust and when you die, you will return to the dust." Gen 3:19

In the KJV version of Proverbs 10:16, the word "work" appears as the word "labour". God tells us that "the labour of the righteous tendeth to life:......".

An interesting verse in 2 Cor 6:1 tells us that we are not only to be workers, but we are to be co-workers with Jesus so that the grace we received from God be not in vain.

"We are workers together with God, so we beg you: Do not let the grace that you received from God be for nothing." 2 Cor 6:1

So from the above, we receive one lesson. We simply have no choice, if we are to imitate God, as Paul tells us to do, we have to work and we have to work with him.

2. God's projects usually begin and end, but his other work continues.

God instituted "rest periods" such as at the end of the week and at the end of special occasions such as the important Biblical Feasts.

a) end of the week

"Remember to keep the Sabbath holy. Work and get everything done during six days each week, but the seventh day is a day of rest to honor the Lord your God. On that day no one may do any work; not you, your son or daughter, your male and female slaves, your animals, or the foreigners living in your cities." Ex 20:8-10

"There are six days for working, but the seventh day is a day of rest, a day holy for the Lord. Anyone who works during the Sabbath day must be put to death." Ex 31:15

"You must work for six days, but on the seventh day you must rest

– even during the planting season and the harvest season." Ex 34:21

"You are to work for six days, but the seventh day will be a holy day, a Sabbath of rest to honor the Lord. Anyone who works on that day must be put to death." Ex 35:2

"Let us try as hard as we can to enter God's rest so that no one will fail by following the example of those who refused to obey." Heb 4:11

If you read the last Scripture in context (read the whole fourth chapter), it clearly refers to God's established pattern in the Torah – to work for six days and to rest on the seventh day.

It is also clear from all of these Scriptures that God commands us to work for six days (i.e. you must, you are to, you ought to) and then he commands us to rest on the seventh day. There is quite a seriousness about this command – anyone who works on that day must be put to death. While we do not live any longer in Torah times, we need to continue to take this command seriously.

In addition, we need to take that seventh day of rest "to honor the Lord", not to do things for our own pleasure, not to catch up what we did not complete during the six previous days, but clearly to "honor the Lord".

How many of you who read this take this seriously ? Our western society (economy) has almost totally eliminated this God-given command.

Nevertheless, God's "work ethic", God's "pattern" clearly shines through

– we are to work (must work) for 6 days and rest on the seventh.

b) beginning and end of feasts

A similar pattern is established for the Biblical feasts. Read the whole 23rd chapter of Leviticus as well as :
"You are to have holy meetings on the first and last days of the feast. You must not do any work on these days; the only work you may to is to prepare for your meals." Ex 12:16

Besides the 6-1 pattern, God also works on "projects" (e.g. creation, feasts, etc...). Which project is He currently working on ? From all the prophecies which are currently being fulfilled, maybe we can conclude that He is working on a project called the 'rapture'.

On the other hand, God is eternal and consequently his overall work never ends. So, since we are also eternal, our work (manual and mental or both according to Dr. John Stott – see quote mentioned above) never ends. So much for a set retirement age of 60 or 65...

Our lesson learned : our work during the week (whatever "your" week is) and on special occasions (maybe it would be a good idea to re-institute the Biblical feasts in our church calendars ?) has to end some times (means "keep your Sabbath"). However, as it relates to end of life-time, our work never ends – we continue to work until the Lord calls us home and, I believe, beyond that (more about that in Chapter Seven).

3. God's work is "perfect"

In Deut 32:4, it shows us that God's work is "perfect". ***"He is like a rock; what he does is perfect, and he is always fair. He is a faithful God who does no wrong, who is right and fair." Deut 32:4***

Then in the KJV of Heb 13:21, through the writer of Hebrews, the Lord tells us that He makes us perfect in every good work to do his will, working in us that which is well-pleasing in his sight, through Christ Jesus; to whom be glory for ever and ever. Amen.

Our lesson learned : when we correctly imitate God, we need to strive for perfection (nothing less) – not matter who we work for. Therefore, the question is "Do you evaluate your work at the end of each day, and, if necessary, correct your mistakes that day ? Or are you putting it off until the next day ? Or do you say 'nobody knows about it anyway, so forget about it ?"

Are your responses in line with God's Word above ?

This part of God's attribute of "work ethic" goes way beyond what we can imagine. In the second manual, currently in progress, we carefully look at your style of work. In a very specific rating exercise, we pose the following questions :

- If I saw that people in my company were going to do something in an unethical or
- illegal manner, I would stand up and voice objections.
- I set limits to the amount of time and energy I put into my job, and my schedule

- reflects those limits.
- Have you have pilfered supplies?
- Have you ever used the company phone to make personal long-distance phone calls or other calls for that matter on company time ?
- Have you ever taken too much time for lunch ?
- Have you ever falsified or exaggerated information on a resume?
- Have you ever participated in a bribe or kickback ?
- Have you ever charged personal expenses on the company expense account ?
- Have you ever cheated on your income tax and not included ministry income as taxable income ?
- Have you ever lied to a customer?

- Have you ever called in sick when not sick ?

Many of your answers to these questions will point to God's perfection or your imperfection.

4. God's work is either "good" or "very good"

The term "good" in relation to God's work is used in the book of Genesis.

"God named the dry land 'earth' and the water that was gathered together 'seas'. God saw that this was good." Gen 1:10

"So, God created the large sea animals and every living thing that moves in the sea. The sea is filled with these living things, with each

one producing more of its own kind. He also made every bird that flies, and each bird produced more of its own kind. God saw that this was good." Gen 1:21

In Genesis 1:27, God creates human beings in His image. And in Gen 1:31, he uses the term "very good".

"God looked at everything he had made, and it was very good." Gen 1:31

One lesson learned : when we work we need to imitate God in His work and make sure that it is at least "good". And at the end of each task, or when we work with other people (humans), we make sure that it is at least "very good". God, in fact, tells us that we are to become followers (imitate) of what is "good" :

"If you are trying hard to do good, no one can really hurt you." 1 Pet 3:13

In the KJV of Heb 13:21, the Lord also gives us a hint that following what is "good" needs to be combined with what is "perfect" – Make you perfect in every good work to do his will, working in you that which is well-pleasing in his sight, through Jesus Christ; to whom be glory for ever and ever. Amen.

And finally :

5. Not only do we have to work, but we have to do "greater works" than God.

"I tell you the truth, whoever believes in me will do the same things that I do. Those who believe will do even greater things than these, because I am going to the Father." John 14:12

These words by Jesus are astounding and many of us do not understand the possibilities. As Jesus left the earth to sit on the right hand of the Father, he is constantly interceding as the one and only intercessor with the Father. Whatever we ask, in His Name, the Father will grant it. That is what makes "greater works" possible.

Weekly church service after weekly church service, believers are sitting in the pews and are waiting......and waiting.....and waiting......., and waiting.

They are not told (by their spiritual leaders) that they should mimic, should imitate, should follow their spiritual leaders who are following (imitating) Christ. Those spiritual leaders are (should be) working hard. After all, that's what the Lord showed us in His Word in this Lesson.

Spiritual leaders need and should understand "The Theology of Work". It is true that one is not saved by works, but by faith and through the grace of God. However, we need to tell our followers that once saved, we need to start working and what Paul tells us in 1 Cor 11:1, it has to start with us.

REPETITION IS THE MOTHER OF ALL LEARNING

Listening/Viewing Assignment – in order to further strengthen your learning of this topic, teaching through a DVD series is available to the readers. Please check in the back of this book for a form to order a copy of this DVD recording.

****

But if, on the other hand, the main purpose of life is seen as extending God's kingdom, a whole raft of activities – loving God, loving people, witnessing, building community, seeking justice, feeding the hungry, caring for creation, working with other to produce goods and services for all to use, doing good works and,

of course, building the church – are all seen as valid parts of life. In such a scenario secular workers feel a sense of 'belonging and significance' within the church and will stay with both the church and their secular work. "Both/and" usually works a lot better than "Eitheror".

Julian Doorey

****

Lesson Six

WWJD ?

Reading Assignment – Read Part II – Foundations for Kingly Motivations, Chapters 7 – 9, and Conclusion in *"Releasing Kings for Ministry in the Marketplace"* by John S. Garfield and Harold R. Eberle, pages 51 – 101

- **Marketplace ministry and the role of Kings in advancing the Kingdom of God is based upon key theological concepts in three areas. Which three ?**

_____

_____

_____

_____

_____

_____

- **The true covenant we have with God is much more than a legal contract. Explain this briefly.**

_____

_____

_____

_____

_____

_____

- **Briefly explain the Theology of Personal Initiative ?**

_____

_____

_____

_____

_____

_____

- **Can you sketch the Worldview of the Progressive Eschatology?**

_____

_____

_____

_____

_____

_____

"Follow my example, as I follow the example of Christ." 1 Cor11:1

In Lesson Four we read – if the instruction in 1 Cor 11:1 was not directly received from Jesus, it was certainly received by inspiration of the Holy Spirit as all Scriptures are inspired by the Holy Spirit.

Follow me as I follow the example of Christ is easily solved by studying "the example of Christ" in the Scriptures. Paul, either through direct contact with Jesus (in visions) or through the inspiration of the Holy Spirit, got a very good handle on "What Would Jesus Do ?"

"But Jesus said, 'I tell you the truth, the Son can do nothing alone. The Son does only what he sees the Father doing, because

the Son does whatever the Father does." John 5:19

So, if we follow Christ's example, we can do nothing alone. We do only what we see Jesus doing, because we do whatever Jesus does. So, we get a whole new perspective on 1 Cor 11:1 – we now can say "Follow my example as I follow the example of Christ who follows the example of the Father".

"I can do nothing alone. I judge only the way I am told, so my judgment is fair. I don't try to please myself, but I try to please the One who sent me." John5:30

Jesus was sent by the Father and He only tries to please the One who sent him. In Matt 28:18-20, Jesus gave us the authority and sent us and we can only try to please the One who sent us. We can do nothing alone.

"I don't need praise from people."
John 5:41

If we follow the example of our spir-itual leaders, who follow the example of Christ, who follows the example of the Father, we do not need praise from people – praise from Jesus and the Father is sufficient.

"So Jesus said to them, 'When you lift up the Son of Man, you will know that I am he. You will know that these things I do are not by my own authority but that I say only what the Father has taught me. The one who sent me is with me. I always do what is pleasing to

***him, so he has not left me alone."
John 8:28-29***

You do nothing by your own authority. You do and say only things by the authority given to you by Jesus (Matt 28:19), who got His authority from the Father (Matt 28:18). Jesus sent you and you always do and say what pleases Him and He will never leave or forsake you (Heb 13:5) and he will always be with you (Matt 28:20).

"So, why do you say that I speak against God because I said, 'I am God's Son' ? I am the one God chose and sent into the world. If I don't do what the Father does, then don't believe me. But if I do what my Father does, even though you don't believe in me, believe what I do. Then you will know and

understand that the Father is in me and I am in the Father." John 10:36-38

If asked about their faith or religion, most Christians might give the name of the denominational group they belong to – I am a Roman Catholic, I am a Presbyterian, I am a Pentecostal, I am an Anglican. Some might say, "I am a Christian". Some might dare to say, "I am a born-again, Spirit-filled believer". Very few might say, "I am a son (or daughter) of God. In fact, if one would say that to unbelievers, they might indeed accuse you of blasphemy as they did in Jesus' time. People would raise their eyebrows and think you belong in some mental institution.

The reality is that, if born again, you are indeed a son or daughter of

God, a brother or sister to Jesus....
So, why would you hide that fact ?

However, we can not live a double life. We can not say that we are a son or daughter of God unless we do what the Father does. So, when is the last time you laid hands on someone and the person received a miracle or healing ? Outsiders, particularly unbelievers, might not be so skeptical if we do what Jesus did – laying hands on the sick and then, in turn, received full miracles and healing. Then you would have the right to say that Jesus (the Father) is in you and that you are in Jesus (the Father).

The real reason why we do not see as many miracles in today's world (and church) is that believers are not doing what the Father does.

"The things I taught were not from myself. The Father who sent me told me what to say and what to teach. And I know that eternal life comes from what the Father commands. So whatever I say is what the Father told me to say." John 12:49-50

If we careful study this Scripture, we can understand what Jesus said in Matt 28:19. In some translations, He tells us to make "disciples" of ALL people in the world. In some translations that means "followers". 1 Cor 11:1 becomes clearer and clearer – follow me as I follow Jesus, who follows the Father. The word "disciples" means "disciplined ones – ones who know what is in the Scriptures, ones who only do what the Father would do. If you are not disciplined and not know what is in the Scriptures, you can NOT do what the Father does.

What is more interesting, maybe even scary, is that Jesus makes the link between doing what the Father does and receiving eternal life. This needs some true reflection....

"Don't you believe that I am in the Father and the Father in me ? The words I say to you don't come from me, but the Father lives in me and does his own work. Believe me when I say that I am in the Father and the Father in me. Or believe because of the miracles I have done." John 14:10-11

Even so-called believers will question you. This Scripture describes Jesus' response to Philip, one of his followers. Even the people (and other leaders in the church) need to see that you are doing what the Father would do, including laying of hands and pray for miracles and healing.

"but the world must know that I love the Father, so I do exactly what the Father told me to do. Come now, let us go." John 14:31

This explains the motivation behind the command to do what the Father does – our love for the Father. We love Him so much that we would do nothing else but what He would do!!! And if we do, the world will know. Our love for the Father prepares the world so that the Father can draw the world to Himself (John 6:44).

So, Paul knew what Jesus was doing – Jesus, through the Scriptures above, said, "Follow me, for I follow the

Father". Paul took this sentiment and said, "Follow me, for I follow Christ". Let's do an interesting exercise which will bring the point home to you.

FILL IN THE BLANKS WITH YOUR NAME (NAME OF STUDENT)

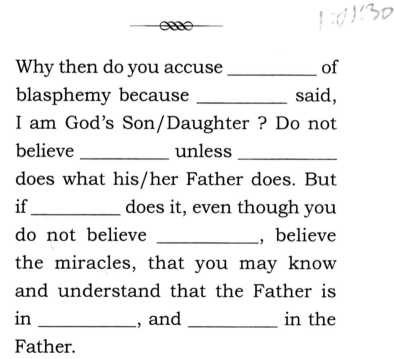

Why then do you accuse _____ of blasphemy because _____ said, I am God's Son/Daughter ? Do not believe _____ unless _____ does what his/her Father does. But if _____ does it, even though you do not believe _____, believe the miracles, that you may know and understand that the Father is in _____, and _____ in the Father.

Don't you believe that _____ is in the Father, and that the Father is in _____ ? The words _____ says to you are not just _____'s own. Rather, it is the Father living in _____, who is doing his work. Believe _____ when _____ says that _____ is in the Father and the Father is in _____ .

_____ gave them this answer, _____ tells you the truth, _____ can do nothing by (him/her) self; _____ can only do what _____ sees the Father doing, because whatever the Father does, _____ also does.

... but the world must learn that _____ loves the Father and that

_____ does exactly what the Father has commanded _____.

_____ can do nothing; _____ judges only as _____ hears, and _____'s judgment is just, for _____ seeks not to please (him/her)self but him who sent _____.

The one who sent _____ is with _____; he has not left _____ alone, for _____ always does what pleases the Father.

_____ does not accept praise from men,...

For _____ did not speak of _____'s own accord, but the Father who sent _____ com-manded _____ what to say and how to say it. Know that his command

leads to eternal life. So whatever
_____ says is just what the
Father has told _____ to say.

****

REPETITION IS THE MOTHER OF ALL LEARNING

Listening/Viewing Assignment – in order to further strengthen your learning of this topic, teaching through a DVD series is available to the readers. Please check in the back of this book for a form to order a copy of this DVD recording.

****

Do you ever feel guilty for going to work when you could be doing ministry instead ? If you're a student, you're

spending hours in the classroom,
hours typing papers,
hours taking tests. But you could
be out evangelizing.
If you're in the workplace, you
spend hours in front
of your computer, hours in
meetings, hours in your little
cubicle. But you could be on the
mission field leading
people to Jesus.

Should you feel guilty ?
I remember hearing a student
leader in college who thought the
answer to that
question was definitely yes.
We were on a retreat,
and he was delivering a
passionate exhortation.
His belief was that God's default
expectation was

for all Christians to go into
full-time vocation ministry
the exception was the
rare person whom
– God called to be in a
– "secular job."

It sounds plausible, doesn't it ?
It's certainly well-intentioned.
But I don't think it's biblical.
Justin Taylor

****

Lesson Seven

"Work from Genesis to Revelation"

Reading Assignment – Read Part III, Attributes of Kings, Motivated for the Marketplace, Chapters 10 – 17, and Conclusion in *"Releasing Kings for Ministry in the Marketplace"* by John S. Garfield and Harold R. Eberle, pages 103 – 147

• **Why did Jesus give us the parable about three men who were entrusted with the property of their master (Matt 25:14-28) ?**

_____

_____

_____

_____

_____

_____

_____

• **Show in a diagram which identity shift Kings undergo ?**

_____

_____

_____

_____

_____

_____

_____

- **Passion leads to real holiness – explain ?**

_____

_____

_____

_____

_____

_____

- **What is the key to answered prayer for Kings ?**

_____

_____

_____

_____

_____

_____

_____

• **The anointing of Kings consists of two elements – which are they?**

_____

_____

_____

_____

_____

_____

_____

• **Do Kings have a limited view of finances and resources? Explain.**

_____

_____

_____

_____

_____

_____

_____

- ***Name three of the six strongholds that must be broken to release Kings into their God-given inheritances ?***

_____

_____

_____

_____

_____

_____

_____

"Follow my example, as I follow the example of Christ." 1 Cor 11:1

From a "Theology of Work" perspective, Paul not only makes this statement, but from my observations he also lived this statement. He wrote almost two thirds of the New Testament as we know it. At the same time he worked as a tent maker, he traveled, preached and taught all over the Middle East and Europe (look at the maps in some Bibles), he ran a Bible School (Acts 19:9), and did much, much more. In today's terms, he certainly would be called a workaholic. But was he ?

No, he was following the example of Christ.

"But Jesus said to them, 'My father never stops working, and so I keep working, too." John 5:17

As a child I used to get "bad" dreams. My dear mom would hold me and tell me "not to worry" and "to put my trust in God the Father as He was watching over me all night". She then prayed and eventually these bad dreams disappeared out of my life and I was able to have a fairly normal sleeping pattern. Not until I studied the Scriptures in detail did I understand my mom's approach to my obvious problem.

See, my Father never stops working, Jesus never stops working. In fact, in Psalm 121:3-4, the psalmist tells us that God ***"will not let your foot slip – he who watches over you will not slumber; indeed, he who watches over Israel will neither slumber nor sleep."*** He is awake all the time, he never stops working. God is clearly a very, very hard worker. Throughout the Scriptures he is identified as having quite a number of various vocations : a shepherd, a king, a potter, a builder, a farmer, a musician, a weaver, and others.

The first two chapters of Genesis give us a very clear picture that God indeed is a very hard worker. The vocation he occupies in those two chapters is the vocation of being a "creator".

In Genesis 1:26, the Father, the Son and the Holy Spirit (us = Trinity) decided to *"make human beings in our image and likeness"*. And immediately, God places man in charge over His creation. He immediately puts man "to work". In Chapter 2 of Genesis, again, he repeats that charge : *"The Lord God put the man in the garden of Eden to care for it and work it." Gen 2:15* In other words, Adam had to take care of the garden and everything in it.

As Adam and Eve were made perfect, they had God-like qualities and to take care of the garden would have been a very easy task. If Adam and Eve would have been obedient, they (and their offspring) would have continued to live in a wonderful, perfect place. They (and their offspring) would have continued to care for the garden and everything in it, using their God-like qualities as they were created in God's image and likeness. Taking care of (working in) a perfect world... But that did not happen! Adam and Eve became disobedient to God and God had no other choice but to stick to his word given in Genesis 2:16-17.

While it was God's intent to create Adam to be in direct fellowship with Him and to become partners in His creative work – asking him to take care of the garden, naming the animals, etc..., it simply did not work out.

So, in Genesis 3:17-19, God deals with the disobedience of Adam : ***"Then God said to the man, 'You listened to what your wife said,*** *and you ate fruit from the tree from which I commanded you not to eat. So, I will put a curse on the ground, and you will have to work very hard for your food all the days of your life. The ground will produce thorns and weeds for you, and you will eat the plants of the field. You will sweat and work hard for your food. Later you will return to the ground, because you were taken from it. You are dust, and when you die, you will return to the dust.*" No more perfect garden but rather weeds in the field, no more God-like qualities to rely on but rather hard work that will produce sweat, no more eternal life in fellowship with God but rather physical death....

On the other hand, prior to speaking to Adam after the Fall, God also speaks to the snake : *"I will*

make you and the woman enemies to each other. Your descendants and her descendants will be enemies. One of her descendants will crush your head, and you will bite his heel." Gen 3:15 God says "My plan for a perfect world is not lost. As of this day, I am putting a plan into motion which will see the restoration of what I intended in the first place." He was going to start a plan to restore everything – our relationship with God, our relationship with others, and our relationship with our environment (creation). The promise was to have, once again, some type of perfect, balanced world in which we could have a wonderful, personal fellowship with God and others – similar again to us walking in the garden of Eden with God on our side.

Immediately after the Fall, God's on-going work (plan) of redemption begins.

After the Fall, from Genesis to Malachi, the Scriptures are filled with real life stories of workers, hard workers. Many of the spiritual lessons to be learned from the Old Testament can be found within "work environments" – testing grounds given by God to allow men and women of faith to develop spiritual character. Here are only a few examples :

Noah
―――――-

"Build a boat of cypress wood for yourself. Make rooms in it and cover it inside and outside with tar. This is how big I want you to build the boat : ..." Gen 6:14-15a)

"Noah did everything that God commanded" Gen 6:22

"Take with you seven pairs, each male with its female, of every kind of clean animal, and take one pair, ..." Gen 7:2a

"Noah did everything the Lord commanded him." Gen 7:5

Though he knew he would be ridiculed by his neighbours, maybe even his family, Noah was obedient and did exactly as the Lord asked him. This obedience resulted in him and his immediate family being saved from the flood.

Obedience to God is Step # One no matter where God places us to work. All of us are given a "sphere of influence" (2 Cor 10:13) and God expects us to be obedient to him within that sphere. As pointed out in the required reading so far, most "spheres" of influence (about 80%) are outside the church (i.e. in the secular world).

Joseph

_____

"But the Lord was with Joseph and showed him kindness and caused the prison warden to like Joseph. The prison warden chose Joseph to take care of all the prisoners, and he was responsible for whatever was done in the prison. The warden paid no attention to anything that was in Joseph's care because the Lord was with Joseph and made him successful in everything he did." Gen 39:21-23

Here we see Joseph in a prison of a society that did not believe in the God of Joseph (our God) and still he was chosen by the prison warden to take care of all the prisoners. In fact, he was made responsible for whatever was done in the prison. He was so good at his job that the warden did not pay attention to anything that Joseph was doing.

Joseph kept close to his God (our God) and because of this, he was able to work hard and perform perfectly in a very difficult work environment.

So, the line between the secular and the sacred is very thin. If we work in a secular environment (the sphere God has assigned to us), we are to keep close to God. And if we keep close to God, we will be able to perform perfectly, even to the point that our employer will put us in charge. If then asked how you did such a wonderful job, it opens up an exciting door to witness...

If the Lord gives us that "sphere of influence", if He sends us, He has promised that *"I will be with you always, even until the end of this age." Matt 28:20*

Nehemiah

―――――――――

"So we rebuilt the wall to half its height, because the people were willing to work." Neh 4:6

"It took fifty-two days to rebuild. When all our enemies heard about it and all the nations around us saw it, they were shamed. They then understood that the work had been done with the help of our God." Neh 6:15b-16

Nehemiah made it quite clear that willingness is also a necessary ingredient. What the priest Ezra could not accomplish in years, Nehemiah, in a kingly function, and the people were able to do in fifty-two days.

The mixture of a willingness to work and the presence of God caused a true miracle.

Daniel
———————

"So *those four young men became the king's servants. Every time the king asked them about something important, they showed much wisdom and understanding.*

They were ten times better than all the fortune-tellers and magicians in his kingdom." Dan 1:19b-20

The same theme given to us in Genesis through the life of Joseph is repeated here in Daniel. Those four men were in an environment hostile to the Living God (our God). However, because of the obedience of the four young men, and the presence of God (our God) in their lives, their work performance was ten times better than the usual workers in the palace.

Jesus, warning us against false prophets in Matt 7:15-20, He tells us that false or good prophets shall be known by their fruits (bad or good fruit). Likewise, when we are given a sphere of influence by God, we shall be known by the fruit we produce. We really need to hear this : "Look what so and so is doing. His work is excellent. How did He do it!!!"

Zechariah

_____

"This is what the Lord All-Powerful says: 'Work hard, you who are

hearing these words today. The prophets spoke these words when the foundation was laid for the house of the Lord All-Powerful, for the building of the Temple." Zech 8:9

"Judah and Israel, your names have been used as curses in other nations. But I will save you, and you will become a blessing. So don't be afraid; work hard." Zech 8:13

Even if our names are pulled through the mud (see Judah and Israel), even if we might be ridiculed (see Noah), the Lord commands us to "work hard". He then promises us to save us, and to make us a blessing (even to the secular world). So don't be afraid, work hard!!!!

The prophets, the kings, the judges and the hard workers described above all played a key role in God's plan of redemption and they showed it mainly through the work they were doing for God. God simply asked them to become key players in His great plan and they were obedient to his call.

And then Jesus comes unto the scene (Luke 2:7).

Except for what is described in Luke 2:41-52 (the story of 12 year old Jesus), very little else is told in the Scriptures about Jesus as a child, as a teenager, or as a young adult. We know that He lived with his parents, Mary and Joseph, in a town called Nazareth. He was described as the "carpenter's son". ***"He is just the son of a carpenter." Matt 13:55a*** However, we also know that ***"The little child grew and became***

strong. He was filled with wisdom, and God's goodness was upon him." Luke 2:40

To fully understand how Jesus grew up is to understand Jewish culture, geography and climate. It is almost certain that Jesus, as the firstborn of the family, learned the vocation of his (step)father Joseph. That means that most of past artists' renderings of Jesus are, most likely, not very accurate. His brown to dark brown skin was wrinkled

through exposure to the warm sun and wind as carpenters in the Middle East, even until today, work outside their shops making furniture or construction lumber. Jesus had broad shoulders from carrying lumber. He had strong muscles, calluses on his hands and his feet – in fact, he, most probably, looked like a rough, tough carpenter – like a hard-working construction worker... His three years of public ministry were filled with observations of daily activities within the community seen through the eyes of an ordinary hard-working carpenter. He always, even within the parables, used very practical examples of daily living. After studying the four Gospels, there is absolutely no doubt that Jesus appreciated the lives of the "workers" within his own community and the communities he visited (i.e. farmers, shepherds, fishermen, women drawing water at local wells, some priests, soldiers, civil servants).

"I give you a new command: Love each other. You must love each other as I have loved you. All people will know that you are my

followers if you love each other." John 13:34-35

This is what he wanted those ordinary workers to add to their daily lives : to follow Him and to love each other. Later in Matthew, he explains what this means : *"I was hungry, and you gave me food. I was thirsty, and you gave me something to drink. I was alone and away from home, and you invited me into your house. I was without clothes, and you gave me something to wear. I was sick, and you cared for me. I was in prison, and you visited me." Matt 25:35-36*

He did not say become a social ministry worker. He did not say : become priests in the church and once you are a priest, you have to start a ministry in the church to feed the hungry, to give clothes to the poor, to visit the prisoners, etc... It is interesting to note that Matt 25 has been used by church institutions and para-church organizations to create large money making ministries that employ (pay fantastic salaries to) ministry workers. As noble as it sounds, I do not believe that this was the intention of Jesus' remarks in Matt 25. I believe that he wanted ordinary workers, ordinary citizens in the community to start following Him and to witness for Him within the spheres of influence He gave them by doing all those things mentioned in Matt 25, and consequently become effective witnesses for Him.

Just before He leaves us, Jesus commands us again to go into the world and to make disciples for (followers of) Him – to teach them everything He taught us, including the lessons from Matt 25, and including the obvious appreciation He had for ordinary workers and the work they were doing.

So, the work of redemption was completed on the cross by Jesus but He charged us with the task to bring that good news to others who do not know. Our new birth experience made us sons and daughters of the King, and the King wants us to "work" with Him (co-workers with Him) in and for the benefit of the Kingdom.

The rest of the Scriptures (Acts, the Epistles, Revelation) give us both instructions on how to work for Him in the Kingdom as well as prophecies how the whole plan of redemption is going to be finally wrapped up by our Master and King.

The Apostles Paul and James are the ones who have probably the most to say about the issue of "work" within the New Testament. More about that in Lesson Eight.

Reviewing the concept of "work" from Genesis to Revelation shows us that the concept of work is and always will be of extreme importance in the heart and mind of God. In fact, it is part of His nature – one of His attributes. So what are we to expect when we go to heaven, when we go to be with Him for eternity.

The prophet Isaiah gives us a wonderful picture on what it is going to be like. The Holy Spirit wanted Isaiah to pen down a little foretaste of heaven. While the scholars attribute the following prophecy to the Millenium reign with Jesus, it shows us accurately what to expect : ***"Look, I will make new heavens and a new earth, and people will not remember the*** *past or think about those things. My people will be happy forever because of the things I will make. I will make a Jerusalem that is full of joy, and I will make her people a delight. Then I will rejoice over Jerusalem and be delighted with my people. There will never again be heard in that city the sound of crying and sadness. There will never be a baby from that city who lives only a few days. And there will never be an older person who doesn't have a long life. A person who lives a hundred years will be called young, and a person who dies before he is a hundred will be thought of as a sinner. In that city those who build houses will live there. Those who plant vine-yards will get to eat their grapes. No more will one person build a*

house and someone else live there.
One person will not plant a garden
and someone else eat its fruit. **My**
people will live a long time, as
trees live long. My chosen people
will live there and enjoy the things
they make. *They will never again*
work for nothing. **They will never**
again give birth to children who
die young. All my people will be
blessed by the Lord; they and their
children will be blessed. *I will pro-*
vide for their needs before they
ask, and I will help them while
they are still asking for help.
Wolves and lambs will eat together
in peace. Lions will eat hay like
oxen, and a snake on the ground
will not hurt anyone. They will not
hurt or destroy each other on all
my holy mountain, says the Lord."
Isa 65:17-25

Millenium or not, heaven or not, this rendition, given by God to Isaiah, gives us hope. This will be a wonderful place – a place where we will be reigning with Jesus. A very special place.... Look careful at the underlined verses within this passage.

This place does not speak about littlle angels with wings flying around. It does not speak about perpetual praise and worship in front of God's throne (though I believe there will be a place where that will happen). Look careful at the underlined verses within this passage. We will be building houses and live in them. We will be planting vineyards and eat the produce. And we will still have needs. We will still pray to God and ask Him to fulfill our needs. However, He will answer our prayer requests before we pray them.

Building houses and planting vine-yards sounds to me like "working".

Working in the new heavens and the new earth ? Working ?

REPETITION IS THE MOTHER OF ALL LEARNING

Listening/Viewing Assignment – in order to further strengthen our learning of this topic, teaching through a DVD series is available to the readers. Please check in the back of this book for a form to order a copy of this DVD recording.

****

**Our strategy is to bless the
nations by releasing
an army of Kings having a
mission to change
cultures with the Gospel of Life
more abundantly...
Impart the message,
make the money,
do the mission, and make
more disciples that will
make a difference.
John. S. Garfield**

****

Lesson Eight

What happened on the cross & two more perspectives from James and Paul

Reading Assignment – Read Part IV – The Personal Lives of Kings, Chapters 18 – 25, and Conclusion in *"Releasing Kings for Ministry in the Marketplace"* by John S. Garfield and Harold R. Eberle, pages 149 – 200

- **God is not looking for robots to carry out His plans mindlessly. What is He looking for ?**

_____

_____

_____

_____

_____

_____

_____

- **What do religious traditions do to people ?**

_____

_____

_____

_____

_____

_____

_____

- *List five steps to remain child-like ?*

_____

_____

_____

_____

_____

_____

_____

- *What is a common failure scenario if you have a kingly calling as most of us do ?*

_____

_____

_____

_____

_____

_____

_____

- **What is key to connect with the unwilling ?**

_____

_____

_____

_____

_____

_____

- **The real goal of godly leader-ship is to connect people with three simple things ?**

_____

_____

_____

_____

_____

_____

_____

- **Name two things that connect Kings to the mentoring
  process?**

_____

_____

_____

_____

_____

_____

- **In Deuteronomy we notice that
  God deals with sin to the third
  and fourth generation, but
  something else to a thousand
  generations. What is that ?**

_____

_____

_____

_____

_____

_____

- ***What does Marketplace
  Ministry provide ?***

_____

_____

_____

_____

_____

_____

_____

*"When Jesus tasted the vinegar,
he said, 'It is finished.' Then he
bowed his head and died." John
19:30*

So what was finished ? Do you
remember Lesson Seven ? Immediately
after the Fall, God put a plan into
action (Gen 3:15) and from Gen 3:15
until Matt 1:1 this plan unfolds but
is well summed up by John : ***God
loved the world so much that he***

gave his one and only Son so that whoever believes in him may not be lost, but have eternal life. God did not send his Son into the world to judge the world guilty, but to save the world through him. People who believe in God's Son are not judged guilty. Those who do not believe have already been judged guilty, because they have not believed in God's one and only Son. They are judged by this fact : The Light has come into the world, but they did not want light. They wanted darkness, because they were doing evil things. All who do evil hate the light and will not come to the light, because it will show all the evil things they do. But those who follow the true way come to the light, and it shows that the things

they do were done through God."
John 3:16-21

Most preachers and teachers stop at the end of the sixteenth verse and do not go on. However, what follows verse sixteen is of crucial importance. In verse twenty-one it states that "those who follow the true way come to the light and it (the light = Jesus) shows that the things they do were done through God. That's quite important to understand.

Salvation means much more than Jesus dying for your sins. I also means that you are saved from your enemies and from slavery of any kind. That you receive health and all kinds of deliverance but, more importantly, you receive the final and complete deliverance from the curse (see Genesis 3) including death. On the cross, Jesus brought us, who believe in Him by faith and through the grace of God, full deliverance over death. This means complete restoration of all that God intended in the first place – a "garden of Eden" where mankind can live in harmony and peace together, side by side with God. This is exactly what is described in Isaiah 65:17-25.

And now knowing that the concept of "work" is not only embraced by God but is actually one of God's own attributes, that concept will be part of the new heavens and the new earth.

The Apostles James and Paul, within their respective epistles, elaborate quite extensively on the concept of work.

a) James

"Do what God's teaching says; when you only listen and do

***nothing, you are fooling your-
selves. Those who hear God's
teaching and do nothing are like
people who look at themselves in
a mirror. They see their faces and
then go away and quickly forget
what they looked like. But the
truly happy people are those who
carefully study God's perfect law
that makes people free, and they
continue to study it. They do not
forget what they heard, but they
obey what God's teaching says.
Those who do this will be made
happy.""" James 1:22-25***

James, like Paul in 1 Cor 11:1,
knew that we needed to copy (to imitate) God, according to His Word.
True happiness in life is linked to
study what's in God's Word and then
follow it up by actually doing it. For

instance, the Word says in John 5:17: ***"My father never stops working, and so I keep working, too."*** So, we continue to study this, we meditate on it, we do not forget about it and as it relates to Kingdom building, we "never stop working" either!!!

"My brothers and sisters, if people say they have faith, but do nothing, their faith is worth nothing. Can faith like that save them ?" James 2:14

"In the same way, faith that is alone – that does nothing – is dead." James 2:17

"Some might say, 'You have faith, but I have deeds. Show me your faith without doing anything, and I will show you my faith by what I do. You believe there is one God. Good! But the demons believe

that, too, and they tremble with fear. You foolish person! Must you be shown that faith that does nothing is worth nothing ?" James 2:18-20

"Just as a person's body that does not have a spirit is dead, so faith that does nothing is dead!" James 2:26

After carefully studying James letter, I am sure that James would have been the first one to say that one can only receive salvation through faith and by the grace of God. He would fully agree that one can not receive salvation through works. On the other hand, in the verses above he states that faith without works is dead. He says that any faith action (i.e. prayer, receiving a prophecy, receiving healing, receiving salvation, etc...) needs to be followed by active works. Faith that does nothing is worth nothing..... in fact, it is dead.

b) Paul

"Follow my example, as I follow the example of Christ." 1 Cor 11:1

"And Jesus said to them, 'My father never stops working, and so I keep working, too." John 5:17

Jesus follows the example of His (our) Father. Paul follows the example of Jesus who follows the example of His (our) Father. We follow the example of Paul and our spiritual leaders as they follow the example of Jesus, who follows the example of their (our) Father.

In previous lessons, we learned that God gives us a "sphere of influence" in which we need to work for Him.

"Each one of you should stay the way you were when God called you." 1 Cor 7:20 The KJV states it a little clearer : *"Let every man abide in the same calling wherein he was called."* We need to serve Jesus wherever He has called us, wherever He has placed us... Jesus has called all of us to "serve Him", to "be obedient to Him", to "spread the Gospel" and He, through Paul, tells us that we should be doing that wherever he has placed us.

"In all the work you are doing, work the best you can. Work as if you were doing it for the Lord, not for people. Remember that you will receive your reward from the Lord, which he promised to his people.

You are serving the Lord Christ."
Col 3:23-24

God places us sometimes in the most humble place. At times we wonder why we are where we are. At times we wonder why we are doing what we are doing. However, the Lord tells us to do what we are doing for the Lord, and not for people. And He promises us that He will reward us no matter if our worldly compensation might seem ridiculous.

"Because of this, since the day we heard about you, we have continued praying for you, asking God that you will know fully what he wants. We pray that you will also have great wisdom and understanding in spiritual things so that you will live the kind of life that honors and pleases the Lord

in every way. You will produce fruit in every good work and grow in the knowledge of God." Col 1:9-10 In the Message Bible (Eugene Peterson), that same verse is translated as follows : *"As you learn more and more how God works, you will learn how to do your work."*

Most of Paul's writings instruct us to do exactly that – to enable us to learn how God works, to learn about God's work ethic. No wonder He tells us to follow his example as he follows God's example.

"Those who are stealing must stop stealing and start working. They should earn an honest living for themselves. Then they will have something to share with those who are poor." Eph 4:28

When I was typing this quote, the Lord reminded me of His word in Malachi 3:8 : ***"Should a person rob God ? But you are robbing me."*** If the Lord is asking us to do something and we are not doing it, is that not, in a sense, robbing Him ? We know with certainty that it is sin (James 4:17). Work and working is part of God's make-up (read Lesson Five again). We are to imitate Him, we know that this is the right thing to do. If you don't, you are sinning and, in fact, you are robbing Him.

"Brothers and sisters, by the authority of our Lord Jesus Christ we command you to stay away from any believer who refuses to work and does not follow the teaching we gave you. You yourselves know that you should live as we live. We

were not lazy when we were with you. And when we ate another person's food, we always paid for it. We worked very hard night and day so we would not be an expense to any of you. We had the right to ask you to help us, but we worked to take care of ourselves so we would be an example for you to follow. When we were with you, we gave you this rule : 'Anyone who refuses to work should not eat.' We hear that some people in your group refuse to work. They do nothing but busy themselves in other people's lives. We command those people and beg them in the Lord Jesus Christ to work quietly and earn their own food. But you, brothers and sisters, never become tired of doing good. If some people do not obey what we tell you in

this letter, then take note of them. Have nothing to do with them so they will feel ashamed. But do not treat them as enemies. Warn them as fellow believers." 2 Thess 3:6-15

When Paul started writing his second letter to the church in Thessalonica, he was informed about the behavior of some in the church. He was really disturbed about them. They simply refused to work. They were totally lazy. And for those of you who believe that it only had to do with "spiritual laziness", you are mistaken. Maybe it had something to do with their spiritual lives, but I believe that it had more to do with general laziness – even to the point of not tithing because they did not work in the world – so they did not have anything to tithe to even pay for visiting ministers.

Those who take on this attitude – the opposite of God's attribute of work – should be warned. We are to temporarily shun them (not treat them as enemies) so that they come to their senses.

In this letter, Paul reminds us again of the principle we originally started with in this course : ***"so we would be an example for you to follow."***

REPETITION IS THE MOTHER OF ALL LEARNING

Viewing/Listening Assignment - in order to further strengthen your learning of this topic, teaching through a DVD series is available to the readers. Please check in the back of this book for a form to order a copy of this DVD recording.

****

Everything about you is to be involved in loving God. It makes sense that your work must be involved as well. Just think about how much of your heart, soul and might go into your work. Imagine then, as you spend yourself at that task, being able to say, 'I'm here to do something God wants done, and I intend to do it because I love Him.' The person who can make this statement has turned his work into one of his primary means of obeying the greatest of God's commandments.

Doug Sherman & William Hendricks

****

Lesson Nine

Review of Theology of Work – Marketplace Ministry 201 – Self-Examination Module

After successful completion of Theology of Work – Marketplace Ministry 101, you will be ready to proceed to the Self-examination Module called Theology of Work – Marketplace Ministry 201 (currently under development).

Now understanding concepts such of "being co-workers with Him", "God's work ethic", "how to work within your sphere of influence", and how all of these concepts intertwine with the principles of The Lausanne Covenant, you need to examine yourself in preparation of the "real" work to be done. The Self-examination Module will provide the student with a basic, elementary understanding of correct self-examination based on Biblical truth. Upon completion, the student should be "ready" to effectively work in the world as a "marketplace minister" assisting Jesus with the building of His church.

The Module will give you :

- Biblical foundations of self-examination
- Practical assignments to examine oneself
- Real life examples and case studies on the application of Marketplace Ministry Principles

Comments regarding this book can be addressed to :

Rev. John Fryters, Ph.D., ICADC (ret)
Transition Adviser
CHAKAM School of the Bible Inc.
329 - 38th Street East
Prince Albert – Saskatchewan – S6W
   1A5
Canada
Tel/fax : 306-763-5014
E-mail : *campus@inet2000.com*
Web : *www.worldoutreach.ca*

All profits derived from the sale of this book and the associated DVD series will be designated 100% to the overseas campuses of CHAKAM School of the Bible.

Lesson Ten

Review Questions and Syllabus Answer Keys

Lesson One

——————————-

1. How do we deny our calling and fail in our mission ?

We denied our calling and failed in our mission by becoming conformed to the world or by withdrawing from it.

2. To whom is the message of the Bible addressed ?

The message of the Bible is addressed to all men and women.

3. What does it mean to proclaim Jesus as "The Savior of the world"?

To proclaim Jesus as "The Savior of the world" is not to affirm that all people are either automatically or ultimately saved, still less to affirm that all religions offer salvation in Christ. Rather it is to proclaim God's love for a world of sinners and to invite everyone to respond to him as Savior and Lord in the wholehearted personal commitment of repentance and faith.

4. What is evangelism itself ?

Evangelism itself is the proclamation of the historical, biblical Christ as Savior and Lord, with a view to persuading people to come to him personally and so be reconciled to God.

5. As it relates to social concern, why do some of us have to express penitence ?

Some of us have to express penitence both for our neglect and for having sometimes regarded evangelism and social concern as mutually exclusive.

6. With what should the "church" not be identified ?

The church is the community of God's people rather than an institution, and must not be identified with any particular culture, social or political system, or human ideology.

7. By what has our testimony sometimes be marred ?

Our testimony has sometimes be marred by sinful individualism and needless duplication.

Lesson Two
_____-

8. Why should churches and para-church agencies engage in constant self-examination ?

They should engage in constant self-examination to evaluate their effectiveness as part of the Church's mission.

9. What is our main goal ?

Our main goal should be by all available means and at the earliest possible time, that every person will have the opportunity to hear, understand, and receive the good news.

10. In the past, what did missions export with the gospel and what was the result ?

Missions have all too frequently exported with the gospel an alien culture and churches have sometimes been in bondage to culture rather than to Scripture.

11. What kind of training programs need to be developed for pastors and laity ?

Training programs that do not rely on any stereotyped methodology but should be developed by creative local initiatives according to biblical standards.

12. What does it mean "not to be immune to worldliness of thought and action"?

It means not to surrender to secularism.

13. Freedom of thought, conscience, to practice and propagate religion should be according to these two things ?

According with the will of God and as set forth in the Universal Declaration of Human Rights.

14. What is a church that is not a missionary church ?

A church that is contradicting itself and quenching the Spirit.

15. What needs to happen between Christ's ascension and return?

The interim period is to be filled with the mission of the people of God, who have no liberty to stop before the end.

Lesson Three

_____

16. According to the Founder of Elijah House, John Sanford, what does "Releasing Kings for Ministry in the Marketplace" aims to do ?

Releasing Kings for Ministry in the Marketplace aims to set free the vast army of the Lord's servants to be who they are, God's sons and daughters who partner with Him in building the Kingdom in the world.

17. What is the real work of the ministry and how is it done ?

The real work of the ministry is in the marketplace; it's the saints who take up the mantle of "Kings" who will carry the great commission into all the world.

18. After reading the introduction, give a short description of the contemporary version of the word "King"?

Kings possess the personality, calling, gifting, and ministry to reach the hearts of our cities and all of society. They are bold, creative, competitive and will embrace a personal God who shares His business with Kings.

Lesson Four
_____

19. Who are "Kings" and what is the intended role of Kings ?

Kings are Christians in the marketplace, and have a role out in the world, expanding the Kingdom of God.

Lesson Five

20. In what capacity did Nehemiah achieve what Ezra could not accomplish ?

What Ezra could not accomplish by himself as a Priest was achieved easily by Nehemiah in a "kingly" capacity.

21. Name briefly four characteristics of Kings ?

The Lord chose the Kings. They are cautioned against materialism and other indulgences. They are cautioned to stay close to Scripture. Kings command the people.

22. Name four things that make a King tick ?

a) a business mind-set; b) a competitive spirit; c) motivated by profit; d) creativity and craftsmanship;

e) covenant wealth; f) wisdom and reputation; g) reaching cities

23. Pastors function primarily in _____ and Kings in _____ ?

Pastors (in the church) and Kings (in the marketplace)

24. Give two real examples of "Kings" in the New Testament ?

Peter, the businessman and Paul, the tent maker.

25. When will we receive a return on our investments (quote Scripture) ?

The Kingdom of God offers a huge rate of return on investment. "I tell you the truth," Jesus said to them., "no one who had left home or wife or brothers or parents or children for the sake of the kingdom of God will fail to receive many times as much in this age and, in the age to come, eternal life." Luke 18:29-30

Lesson Six

_____

26. Marketplace ministry and the role of Kings in advancing the Kingdom of God is based upon key theological concepts in three areas. Which three ?

a) Who is God ? b) Who is man ? c) What does the future hold ?

27. The true covenant we have with God is much more than a legal contract. Explain this briefly.

It is a relational commitment. The parties are committed to make decisions together and for the benefit of one another. The covenant allows both parties to enter into the decision-making process. The covenant is a commitment to cooperate and work with each other. God honors and receives the input of His partners on a greater and more intimate level.

28. Briefly explain the Theology of Personal Initiative ?

When we think about work associates (saved or unsaved) we must see them as precious to God. They really are generous, helpful, polite, hard-working, creative, fun-loving, and delightful. Sure, they have some quirks, too. But we need to help all people through life successfully because that is what Jesus would do. They get healed when we pray for them. We can love them. God relates to and works with them. Now, we understand that God not only permits us to take initiative,

He expects us to. It's one of our God-like qualities.

29. Can you sketch the Worldview of the Progressive Eschatology ?

The Church with "Priests" equipping in the Temple————The Kingdom with "Kings" expanding the dominion of Jesus———- The World, new land yet to be taken, "our inheritance".

Lesson Seven

———————-

30. Why did Jesus give us the parable about three men who were entrusted with the property of their master (Matt 25:14-28) ?

This parable was told to instruct us about our responsibilities while we are here. God will hold us accountable to use whatever He has given to us.

31. Show in a diagram which identity shift Kings undergo ?

Sheep/Slaves/Servants————-
Children/Sons/Heirs———Friends/
Brothers/Kings

32. Passion leads to real holiness – explain ?

Real holiness springs out of the passion and fruit that go with the positive things we naturally and passionately desire to do; things that match the heart of God.

33. What is the key to answered prayer for Kings ?

The key to answered prayer for Kings resides in the desires of their hearts. God is looking for people who share His heart to expand the Kingdom. When God find those people, He grants the desires of their hearts.

34. The anointing of Kings consists of two elements – which are they ?

Their anointing and creativity/wisdom.

35. Do Kings have a limited view of finances and resources ? Explain.

A King's mind-set : abundance is God's will. God intervenes with the "ability to produce wealth," as He promised : "But remember the Lord your God, for it is he who gives you the ability to produce wealth, and so conforms his covenant, which he swore to your forefathers, at it is today." Deut 8:17-18

36. Name three of the six strongholds that must be broken to release Kings into

their God-given inheritances ?

a) the resource pie is a fixed quantity; b) It is spiritual to be poor; c) The wealthy are arrogant; d) God automatically will transfer wealth in the last days; e) Businesspeople are not as spiritual as people in full-time ministry; f) Priests have the vision, while Kings have the provision;

Lesson Eight

---

37. God is not looking for robots to carry out His plans mindlessly. What is He looking for ?

He is looking for those who will be bonded to Him in love. "In that day, 'declares the Lord', you will call me 'my husband'; you will no longer call me 'my master'" Hos 2:16

38. What do religious traditions do to people ?

Religious traditions keep people enslaved.

39. List five steps to remain child-like ?

a) Laughter; b) Ask and receive; c) Pretend; d) Play; e) Have a dream.

40. What is a common failure scenario if you have a kingly calling as most of us do ?

The common failure scenario is to idolize the pulpit ministry in their local church or the traveling ministry at the conference or on TV. If you happen to have a kingly calling (most of us do), God isn't calling you to run away from your vocation. He knew all about your vocation before you got saved. He's planting people throughout our cities in business, education, the arts, and government so that all the bases are covered and He touches every corner with His Spirit.

41. What is key to connect with the unwilling ?

Caring about connecting first and promoting their agenda second.

42. The real goal of godly leadership is to connect people with three simple things ?

The real goal of godly leadership is to connect people with three simple things : a) your "kairos" moment; b) your destiny; c) your obedience.

43. Name two things that connect Kings to the mentoring process?

Kings who are successful in their endeavors are the first to point to their mentors. They fondly speak of that molding process and the respect and love they have for the people who first took them by their hands to train them. Kings understand the importance of mentoring from their own experiences. They tend to be generous and willing to share their experiences with the next generation that follows. Kings maintain mentoring relationships throughout their lives.

Kings are always participants in some kind of fraternity of relationships that helps their creative processes and improves the quality of their crafts. They enjoy helping their peers increase their successes. So successful is this type of mentoring that some people not familiar with it would consider it "cheating".

44. In Deuteronomy we notice that God deals with sin to the third and fourth generation, but something else to a thousand generations. What is that ?

Notice that God deals with sin to the third and fourth generation, but shows love to a thousand generations. Deut 5:9-10

45. What does Marketplace Ministry provide ?

Marketplace Ministry provides a revolutionary format to fulfill the Great Commission. It facilitates a synergy between Kings and Priests. It enables God's children to take their inheritance.

website:
ReleasingKings.com
- newsletter

BIBLIOGRAPHY

Institute for hope and life.com
Lessons 4-8

3 on Amazon used 3.92+ 3.99)

Garfield, John S., and Eberle, Harold R., ***Releasing KINGS for Ministry in the Marketplace.*** Yakima, Washington: Worldcast, 2004 *12.95*

www.worldcastministries.com

Garfield, John S., ***Desire to Destiny.*** Kenwick, Washington: Releasing Kings, 2007 *12.95*

www.worldcastministries.com

God, ***Bible.*** New Century Version. Dallas: Word, 1988

The Cape Town Commitment
Chris Wright

Sherman, Doug, and Hendricks, William, ***Your Work Matters to God.*** Book and study guide. Colorado Springs: NavPress, 1987

navpress
16 99

12.49 amazon.com paperback
4.00 used (3.99 shipping + .01)

Christ Our Reconciler,
Tim Keller, Rebecca Manley
Pippert, John Piper, etc

The Covenant of Lausanne
p. 25, p. 65, Lesst-3

Universal Declaration of
Human Rights p. 57

DVD ORDER FORM

I would like to order the non-commercial recorded sessions of "Theology of Work – Marketplace Ministry 101" by Dr. John Fryters.

Cost : $ 25.00 (shipping and handling included)

Name :

_____

_____

Address :

_____

_____

_____

_____

Telephone :

_____

E-mail :

_____

_____

Mail request with payment to :

CHAKAM School of the Bible Inc.
329 - 38ᵗʰ Street East
Prince Albert – Saskatchewan

_____

S6W 1A5

CPSIA information can be obtained at www.ICGtesting.com
Printed in the USA
LVOW120507050613

336931LV00001B/3/P